Little Neighbors

CITY SCIENCE

Thomas F. Sheehan

Rourke

Publishing LLC

Vero Beach, Florida 32964

www.rourkepublishing.com

PHOTO CREDITS: Cover, page 9 © DigitalVision; title page and pages 4, 5 ©
P.I.R.; page 6 © Romie Flanagan; pages 10, 16, 17, 18, 20 © L.Stone; pages 11,
13 © Brand X Pictures; page 14 © Canola Council of Canada; page 15 © William
Roesly; page 16 © Breck Kent and Jerry Hennen; page 20 © J.H. "Pete"
Carmichael; page 22 © Manuel Silva

Consulting editor: Marcia S. Freeman

Library of Congress Cataloging-in-Publication Data

Sheehan, Thomas F.
  Little neighbors / Thomas F. Sheehan.
     p. cm. -- (City science)
  Includes bibliographical references and index.
  ISBN 1-59515-408-6 (hardcover)

Printed in the USA

CG/CG

Table of Contents

City Insect Habitats

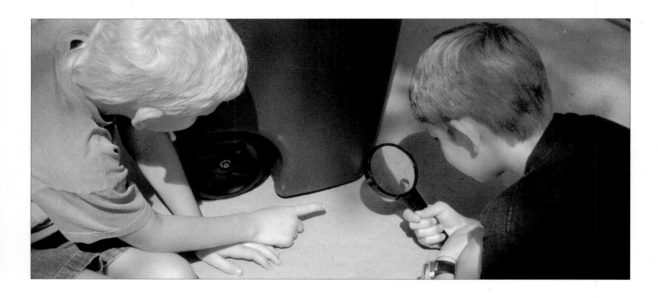

Where do you find insects in the city? You will find them near garbage cans. You will find them on the sidewalks. You will find them flying in the air.

You will find them on plants you grow on your windowsill, balcony, or fire escape. These are insect **habitats**. You can find insects just about anywhere. They are our little neighbors.

Aquatic insects live in ponds and puddles and in streams and swamps. They crawl on the bottom or swim. Some can even walk on the water surface. You can look for aquatic insects in the city. Try a puddle, or a park pond, or a fountain basin.

When you watch or listen to insects you are observing how they live. You should get a **magnifying** glass if you're going to do any serious insect watching. Most insects are pretty small.

City Insect Neighbors

In a city park in the summer you can watch live butterflies flitting from flower to flower. They are sipping the sweet **nectar** with a long, curled mouth tube, called a **proboscis**.

You can learn more about butterflies at a museum of natural history. There you will find collections of insects in display cases.

Insect Bodies

How many wings do you see? How many legs can you count on this insect? Did you know that insects have two feelers on their heads? They are known as antennae.

Some insects can sting, so be careful handling them. It's best to catch them in a net and put them in a little screen cage or plastic container. Then you can safely study them.

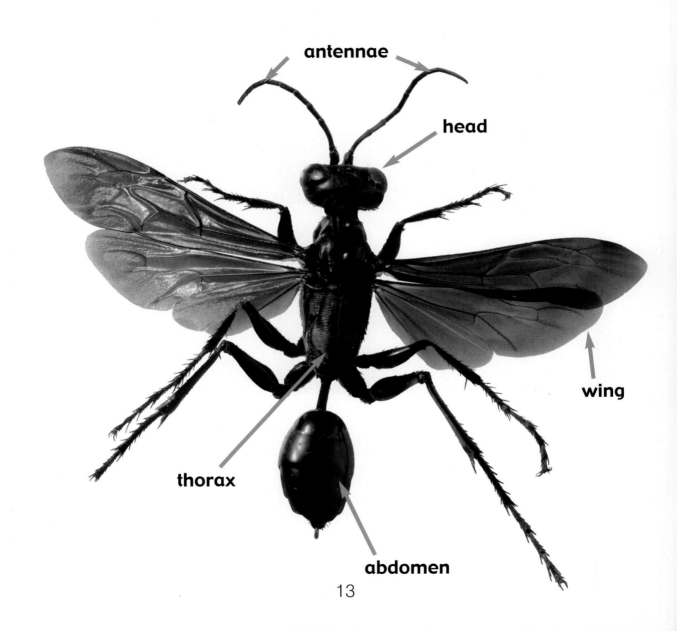

antennae

head

wing

thorax

abdomen

Insect Appetites

Insects eat almost anything that grows. They can find food everywhere, even in a city. That's why insects live everywhere on earth. Just like us!

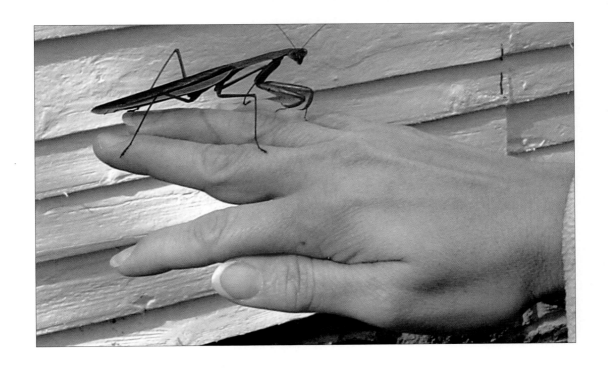

A praying mantis is a very large insect that catches and eats other insects. It feels funny to have it crawl on your skin, but it won't hurt you.

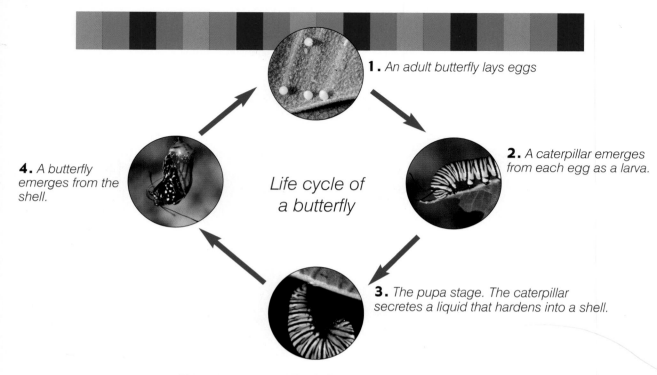

Life cycle of
a butterfly

1. *An adult butterfly lays eggs*

2. *A caterpillar emerges from each egg as a larva.*

3. *The pupa stage. The caterpillar secretes a liquid that hardens into a shell.*

4. *A butterfly emerges from the shell.*

Insect Life Cycles

Insects lay eggs. Houseflies lay their eggs around garbage and smelly, dead stuff. You will find insect eggs on the underside of leaves, on the bark of trees, and other out-of-the-way places. Insect eggs hatch into little, worm-like **larvae**.

Caterpillars are the larvae of butterflies and moths. A larva turns into a **pupa**. You might find a pupa tucked underneath just about anything outside. Look under a windowsill or a slide at the park.

Insects on the Move

Have you ever watched a honeybee crawling on a flower? Bees and other insects crawl, fly, wiggle, and wave their antennae.

Ants carrying a piece of leaf.

Honeybees build honeycombs for their eggs, larvae, and stored food.

Some insects can swim and jump. Some can dig holes, cut leaves, and carry things. Some can build homes for themselves and their **offspring**.

Your Insect Neighbors

Some insects are beautiful and some are not. But all of them are interesting, even a cockroach living under your refrigerator. Keep your eyes open and you will learn what your insect neighbors are doing!

Glossary

aquatic (uh KWAT ik) — living or growing in water
habitats (HAB uh TATS) — places where plants or animals live
larvae (LAR vee) — an early life stage of many insects
magnifying (MAG nuh FY ing) — making something larger to see it better
nectar (NEK tur) — a sweet liquid
offspring (OFF SPRING) — babies
proboscis (pruh BOSS es) — a long curled mouth tube
pupa (PYU puh) — an insect form that comes between the larva and the adult form

Index

Further Reading

Cooper, Jason. *Ants.* Rourke Publishing, 2006
Hartley, Karen et al. *Cockroach.* Heinemann First Library, 1999
Sill, Cathryn. *About Insects:A Guide for Children.* Peachtree, 2000

About The Author

Thomas Sheehan lives, breathes, and teaches science in Maine. He credits the English Departments at Cornell University and SUNY for awakening his interest in good writing, E. B. White's *Elements of Style* for smoothing out the wrinkles, and the editors at *The Bangor Daily News* for discipline.